ENVIRONMENTAL FOOTPRINTS

How Big Is Your Shopping Footprint?

Paul Mason

mc **Marshall Cavendish**
Benchmark

New York

This edition first published in 2010 in the United States of America by Marshall Cavendish Benchmark.

Marshall Cavendish Benchmark
99 White Plains Road
Tarrytown, NY 10591
www.marshallcavendish.us

All Internet sites were available and accurate when sent to press.

First published in 2008 by
MACMILLAN EDUCATION AUSTRALIA PTY LTD
15–19 Claremont Street, South Yarra 3141

Visit our website at www.macmillan.com.au or go directly to www.macmillanlibrary.com.au

Associated companies and representatives throughout the world.

Copyright © Paul Mason 2008

Library of Congress Cataloging-in-Publication Data

Mason, Paul, 1967-
  How big is your shopping footprint? / by Paul Mason.
  p. cm. – (Environmental footprints)
  Includes index.
  ISBN 978-0-7614-4414-5
  1. Environmental responsibility–Juvenile literature. 2. Environmental protection–Citizen participation–Juvenile literature. 3. Green movement–Juvenile literature. 4. Consumer education–Juvenile literature. I. Title.
  GE195.7.M37 2010
  640–dc22

2008048098

Edited by Anna Fern
Text and cover design by Cristina Neri, Canary Graphic Design
Page layout by Domenic Lauricella
Photo research by Legend Images
Illustrations by Nives Porcellato and Andrew Craig

Printed in the United States

Acknowledgments
The author and the publisher are grateful to the following for permission to reproduce copyright material:

Front cover photograph: Earth from space © Jan Rysavy/iStockphoto; colored footprint © Rich Harris/ iStockphoto. Images repeated throughout title.

Photos courtesy of:
AAP/AP Photo/The Oregonian, Paul Kitagaki Jr., **6**; BazuraBagsTM, photo by Rick Fischer, **3** (top right), **27**; © Fintastique/Dreamstime.com, **12**; © Photawa/Dreamstime.com, **20**; © Photointrigue/Dreamstime.com, **21**; © Leah-Anne Thompson/Fotolia, **23**; Gareth Cattermole/Getty Images, **17**; CBS Photo Archive/Getty Images, **25**; Joe Raedle/Getty Images, **13**; James P. Blair/National Geographic/Getty Images, **9**; Karen Moskowitz/Stone/ Getty Images, **11**; Joos Mind/Taxi/Getty Images, **30**; © Jonathan Heger/iStockphoto, **5**; © Andrew Martin Green/iStockphoto, **26**; © starfotograf/iStockphoto, **22**; © Tomasz Trojanowski/iStockphoto, **28**; © Elena Aliaga/ Shutterstock, **16**; © Pieter Janssen/Shutterstock, **14**; © Kuzma/Shutterstock, **24**; © Mirenska Olga/Shutterstock, **7**; © Losevsky Pavel/Shutterstock, **8**; © Supri Suharjoto/Shutterstock, **29**; © Tan Wei Ming/Shutterstock, **19**; © Mark Winfrey/Shutterstock, **18**; © Sherry Yates Sowell/Shutterstock, **10**.

Please note
At the time of printing, the Internet addresses appearing in this book were correct. Owing to the dynamic nature of the Internet, however, we cannot guarantee that all these addresses will remain correct.

1 3 5 6 4 2

Contents

Glossary Words
When a word is printed in **bold**, you can look up its meaning in the Glossary on page 31.

Environmental Footprints

This book is about the footprints people leave behind them. But these are special footprints. They are the footprints people leave on the **environment**.

Heavy Footprints

Some people leave heavy, long-lasting footprints. They do this by:

- acting in ways that harm the environment
- using up lots of **natural resources**, including water, land, and energy

It can be hundreds of years before the environment recovers from heavy footprints.

Light Footprints

Other people leave light, short-lived footprints. They do this by:

- behaving in ways that harm the environment as little as possible
- using the smallest amount of natural resources they can

The environment recovers from light footprints much more quickly.

As the world's population grows, more natural resources will be needed. It will be important not to waste resources if we are to leave light footprints.

The world's population is expected to continue growing in the future.

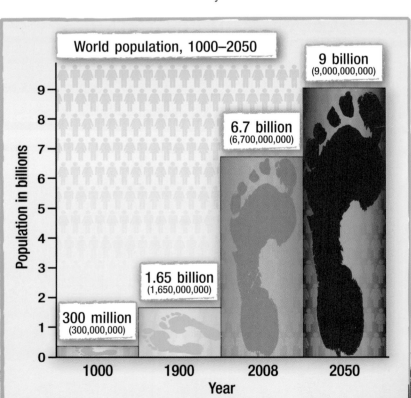

World population, 1000–2050

9 billion (9,000,000,000)

6.7 billion (6,700,000,000)

1.65 billion (1,650,000,000)

300 million (300,000,000)

Population in billions

Year

The environmental effects of transporting goods by truck to where they will be sold is part of a shopping footprint.

What Makes Up a Shopping Footprint?

A shopping footprint is made up of the ways people's shopping affects the environment. Shopping footprints include:

- the raw materials goods are made from
- how the goods are **manufactured**
- how goods are transported
- where goods are sold
- how the goods are **packaged** for sale

Everything people buy affects the environment somehow. The bigger the effect, the bigger the footprint left behind.

What sort of shopping footsteps are you taking? Read on to find out!

The Shopping Industry

The shopping industry is made up of everything involved in the making and sale of the things people buy. Farmers, manufacturers, store owners, and ordinary people all benefit from the shopping industry. But shopping also comes at a cost to the world's environment.

Raw Materials

Raw materials are the things products are made from. For example, cotton T-shirts are made from cotton. Bicycle frames are made from metal. Most manufacturers buy raw materials at the lowest price possible.

Manufacturing

Most goods are manufactured wherever it is cheapest. They are often manufactured in **developing countries**, where **wages** are low. The manufacturer can then choose to sell the goods for a low price, or to sell them at a higher price and make more money. The highest prices can be charged in wealthy countries.

At this factory in Vietnam, thousands of workers make sneakers for a company in the United States.

Transportation

Many goods are transported from developing countries to wealthy countries, where they can be sold for higher prices. Sometimes they travel thousands of miles by train, ship, truck, or even airplane.

Shopping malls are a popular place for people to buy goods.

Packaging

Most products are wrapped up, or packaged, in some way. For example, food is put in colorful cardboard containers. White T-shirts are wrapped in plastic to keep them clean.

Sales

The final stage of a product's journey is for it to be sold. Today, many goods are sold in malls, where lots of big stores are collected together. People can park their cars nearby, walk around the mall, and buy everything they need.

This store offers a large choice of different appliances.

Rethink!

Instead of throwing away old electrical equipment, give it to charity so that it can be used by someone else.

Benefits of the Shopping Industry

The way many goods are manufactured and then sold has great benefits for people, especially in wealthy countries.

- Many goods cost a smaller percentage of people's earnings than ever before. They have been made where wages are lower, so the cost of manufacturing them is lower.

- There is more choice than ever before. Goods can be transported from anywhere around the world, so people are able to buy products made far away. Bigger stores offer a greater choice of products.

- Large shopping malls have made shopping quicker and easier.

Costs of the Shopping Industry

Everything people buy comes at a cost to the environment.

- Growing, manufacturing, and transporting goods uses energy. The energy for all these activities usually comes from burning **fossil fuels**. Burning fossil fuels is one of the ways in which humans are damaging the environment.

- Most manufacturing causes **pollution**. Poisonous chemicals and gases are released into the air and water. They harm the land, plants, and animals.

- Everything people buy uses up natural resources. Some of these cannot be replaced. Once we use up all the petroleum in the world, for example, it will be gone. There will also be no more plastics, **artificial fibers**, or other products made with petroleum.

In 1969, the Cuyahoga River in Cleveland, Ohio, was so polluted with oily waste from manufacturing that its surface caught fire.

Every cent people spend in stores increases the size of their shopping footprint.

Raw Materials and Manufacturing

Everything people buy uses up some sort of natural resource. Using these natural resources often damages the environment, and increases people's environmental footprints.

Nonrenewable Resources

Nonrenewable resources cannot be replaced. Once they have been used up, there will be no more. Nonrenewable resources include many metals, and petroleum, which is used to make plastics. Buying things made from nonrenewable resources increases the size of a person's shopping footprint.

Renewable Resources

Renewable resources can be replaced. Cotton for jeans or T-shirts is renewable—once the cotton has been picked, more can grow. However, growing cotton still affects the environment. Farmers use large amounts of water and poisonous pesticides to grow the plants. Like cotton, many renewable resources harm the environment while they are being produced.

Cotton is a renewable resource, but growing cotton still affects the environment.

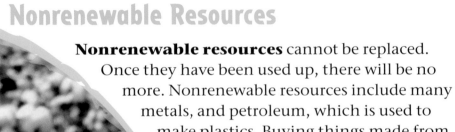

Remodeling old clothes into the latest fashions has a light footprint.

Rethink!

Altering clothes to fit is better for the environment than buying new ones, and has a much smaller environmental footprint.

Manufacturing Goods

Manufacturing means turning raw materials into goods for people to buy. Manufacturing often harms the environment. Paper mills, for example, make paper from wood. The chemicals involved are sometimes released into nearby rivers. They can poison fish, plants, and other living things.

Increasing Demand

The world's demand for products is growing. This is because the world's population is growing, too. Even to have the same effect as we are currently having on the world's environment, each person in the future will have to have a lighter footprint than today.

Reuse

Reusing products instead of buying new ones has a tiny environmental footprint. Buying a secondhand bicycle, for example, means that all the metal, plastic, and rubber that would have been used to make a new one has been saved. The energy that would have been needed to make a new bicycle has been saved, too.

Recycling

Recycling means using the materials contained in old products to make new products. One example of this might be melting down old bicycle frames to make new ones. Recycling has a heavier footprint than reusing. Recycling does not use new raw materials, but it is still a manufacturing process. It uses energy and causes pollution.

Today, almost every kind of material can be recycled.

PLASTIC BOTTLES ONLY

Food and drink cans only

WASTE PAPER ONLY

RECYCLING

Choosing to reuse and recycle goods reduces demand for new products and will give you a lighter shopping footprint.

Case Study

Recycling Cell Phones

The millions of cell phones in the world are not good for the environment. Making the phones uses up resources, and most phones contain poisonous substances such as mercury and cadmium. A discarded battery from one phone can pollute up to 131,981 gallons (600,000 liters) of water.

On average, people get a new phone every 18 months, but only 5 percent of phones were recycled in 2006. Now, though, several charities recycle old phones. The phones are checked over, then sold to new owners.

Recycling phones helps the environment in two main ways.

⊕ The people who use the recycled phones do not have to buy new ones, which saves resources.

⊕ The poisonous substances in the phones are not dumped into the waste system.

People who would rather keep their phones until they no longer work can also recycle them. The broken phones are stripped down and the parts used for repairs.

On Earth Day in Washington, D.C., in 2005, thousands of people donated their old cell phones for recycling.

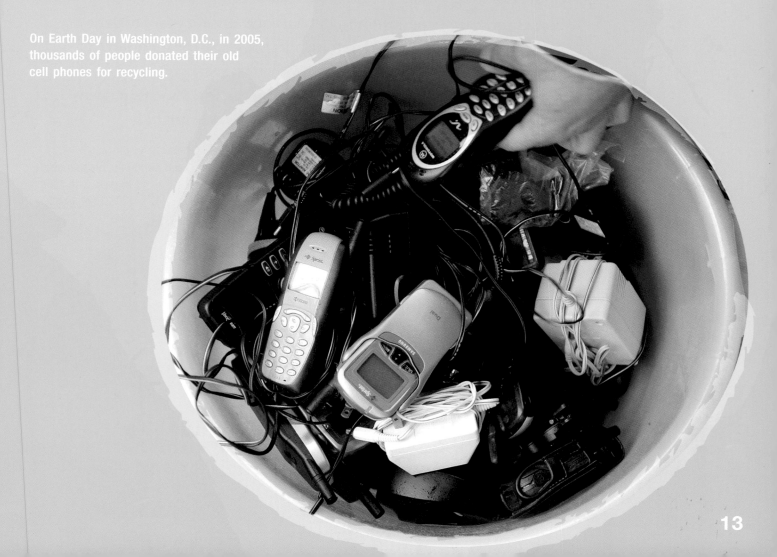

13

Transporting Goods

Transporting goods to where they will be sold harms the environment. How much harm it does depends on how far the goods travel and how they are transported.

Types of Transportation

Goods are usually transported in boats, trains, trucks, or airplanes.

⊕ Boats usually cause the least pollution for every ton of cargo they carry. Boats are often used to transport non-food items, such as cars, bicycles, or electrical goods, over long distances.

⊕ Trains usually cause more pollution than boats, but are a fairly good option for long-distance transportation.

⊕ Trucks cause more pollution than boats or trains for every ton they carry. Trucks are often used to transport goods on the final stage of their journey, to the shops where they will be sold.

⊕ Airplanes cause the most pollution per ton carried. Food that needs to be kept fresh sometimes travels long distances by plane.

Each container on this ship is loaded with tons of goods.

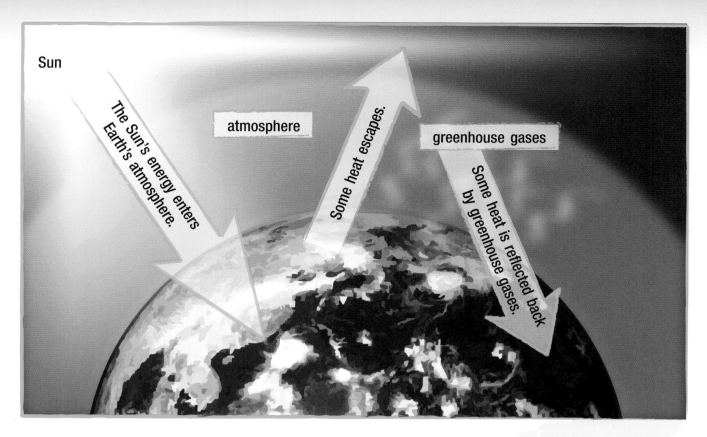

Sun

The Sun's energy enters Earth's atmosphere.

atmosphere

Some heat escapes.

greenhouse gases

Some heat is reflected back by greenhouse gases.

The greenhouse gases produced by transporting goods contribute to global warming.

Effects of Transportation Pollution

When transporting goods causes a lot of pollution, the goods have a heavy environmental footprint. So, lettuce that was grown down the road has a much lighter footprint than lettuce that has to be transported from the other side of the world.

The pollution from transporting goods harms the environment in several ways.

- **Greenhouse gases**, produced by burning fossil fuels to power transportation, are one of the main causes of **global warming**. Global warming is one of the biggest threats to the environment today.

- The pollution that is released by burning fossil fuels also affects the health of humans, animals, and plants.

- Many of the natural resources used to make and run the **transportation system** are nonrenewable and are rapidly being used up.

Rethink!

Food grown in the country where it is sold has a lighter shopping footprint than food from overseas.

Local Products

Products that have been made locally have a lighter footprint than those made far away. Transporting a bicycle frame from nearby causes less transportation pollution than transporting one from farther away, for example.

Local Food

People can reduce the size of their shopping footprints by buying food that has been grown nearby. The environmental effects of transporting food are sometimes called "food miles." Locally grown food has fewer food miles than food transported from far away.

Some food growers, especially **organic farmers**, deliver food right to the customer's door. They deliver food to the customer's door. Others take their crops to **farmers' markets**. In both cases, few food miles are used.

Organic fruit and vegetables from a farmer's market are fresher than goods from far away and have a light footprint.

Choosing to buy goods that have been grown or manufactured near your home will give you a lighter shopping footprint.

Case Study
Ugg Boots

Ugg boots are super-warm boots made of sheepskin. For years, they have been a popular way for surfers to warm up their feet after a cold session. Uggs were originally made by small, local producers in Australia.

Surprisingly (because *ugg* is short for "ugly"), uggs became very fashionable around the world. Sudden fashions like this can be bad for the environment. Factories in developing countries start manufacturing the product, which is then transported all around the world, causing lots of pollution. But ugg boots are made of sheepskin, and sheep can be raised almost anywhere. Buying uggs that are made locally means people can be fashionable and have a lighter footprint, too!

Uggs became fashionable when celebrities such as Kate Moss started wearing them.

Where People Shop

Where and how people shop has a big effect on their shopping footprint. Choosing the right type of store to visit and the right way to get there makes people's shopping footprints lighter.

Shopping Strips and Malls

Shopping strips and malls are increasingly popular places for people to shop. Every year, more are built. These new malls affect the environment, so shopping at them adds to people's shopping footprints.

Building Malls

Building any kind of structure affects the environment. The building materials, such as metal, brick, and glass, are often made from nonrenewable resources. Making the building materials uses up energy, and so does building the shopping mall or strip itself. Energy usually comes from burning fossil fuels, which causes pollution and adds to global warming.

Building new shopping malls uses up a lot of nonrenewable resources.

Energy Consumption in Malls

Once shopping malls have been built, they continue to use up large amounts of energy for lighting, cooling, and heating.

Shops and public areas are lit so that people can easily find their way around. Even when malls close, the lighting usually stays on for security reasons. Energy is used up producing light that no one sees.

Malls keep the temperature inside comfortable for their shoppers. Most of the time, the air is either cooled by air conditioning or warmed by heating. Both use large amounts of energy.

Lighting, cooling, and heating a mall require large amounts of energy.

Rethink!

Outdoor shopping strips use less energy for lighting, heating, and cooling than indoor malls, so they have a lighter environmental footprint.

Traveling to the Store

How people travel to the store affects the size of their shopping footprint. Many new shopping malls and supermarkets are built on the outskirts of town. Most people use their cars to reach these distant stores. This causes more pollution than is necessary.

⊕ A car with two people traveling 4 miles (6.4 kilometers) to the store releases 31.8 ounces (900 grams) of pollution.

If 2,000 people travel 4 miles, two-to-a-car, a total of 31,790 ounces (901,233 g) of pollution is released.

⊕ A bus seating 50 people traveling 4 miles to the store releases 136 ounces (3,862 g) of pollution.

If 2,000 shoppers travel 4 miles to the store (40 busloads of people), a total of 5,450 ounces (154,505 g) of pollution is released. That's less than one-fifth the pollution of the same number of people traveling by car!

If everyone who drove had walked, cycled, or caught the bus, it would have caused much less pollution.

Paving the Land

Forests are often cut down to make room for new stores on the outskirts of cities or towns. This earth is covered in concrete, then stores and parking lots are built. This causes problems for the environment, especially for the local water system.

Before, rain would fall and soak into the soil, or wash into streams and rivers. Once the land is paved, the rainwater cannot soak into the soil. Instead, the heat of the sun causes some of the water to **evaporate**. The rest washes into drainage channels, and then into **sewers**. The water does not replenish local rivers, which is bad for plants, fish, and other animals.

With parking lots covering the land, heavy rain washes into drains instead of soaking into the soil.

Alternative Ways to Shop

Many shoppers are now finding alternative ways to shop that reduce the effect they have on the environment.

Walking and Cycling

One-third of car journeys are less than 1.9 miles (3 km), and lots of these short journeys are to stores. It is easy to walk or cycle this distance. Walking and cycling to stores does not produce pollution.

Internet Shopping

Many people do some of their shopping on the Internet. Internet goods often come from a warehouse, which uses less energy than a shopping mall. The goods are delivered by truck. One truck delivering to 100 customers on one continuous journey causes far less pollution than 100 customers driving to the store.

Internet shopping also allows people to buy and sell secondhand goods easily. Buying secondhand saves on resources used to make new goods.

Walking to the store and taking your own bag has a lighter footprint than driving and using disposable plastic bags.

Choosing to shop in ways that use less energy and with a smaller environmental impact will give you a lighter shopping footprint.

Case Study

Buying Food Online

In the past, people living far from cities often had to drive a long way to buy unusual foods. Today, Internet food shopping provides a good alternative.

Gourmet websites offer people the chance to buy food over the Internet and have it delivered to their door. These sites offer food from all over the country.

For example, honey from Hawaii, orange juice from California, and baked beans from Michigan can all be ordered from one Internet store. This means that the goods each make one journey to the customer. This creates less pollution than buying them from lots of individual stores, so it has a lighter environmental footprint.

Today, almost everything can be bought online.

Packaging and Product Life

Packaging is the wrapping that many products come in. "Product life" describes how long a product lasts. Both have a big effect on people's shopping footprints.

Packaging

Packaging is usually made of paper, cardboard, or plastic. It is used:

⊕ to keep products clean and safe before they are sold

⊕ to keep food fresh

⊕ to make products look more appealing to buyers.

Packaging is made using resources and energy, which are wasted if the packaging is unnecessary

Waste

Packaging that is discarded adds to the world's growing mountain of waste. Up to one-third of nonindustrial waste was once packaging. Much of this takes years to rot away and disappear.

Discarded packaging pollutes the world's beaches.

Product Life

Some products have a longer life than others. One T-shirt might last three months, while another lasts ten years. The reasons for products having a short life include:

- they have worn out
- they have become useless because technology has changed, such as a computer that is too old to run a modern operating system
- they are no longer fashionable

Choosing products that last a long time will give you a lighter shopping footprint.

Rethink!

Disposable plastic shopping bags create waste. Bringing reusable canvas bags to hold your purchases at the mall or grocery store lowers your shopping footprint.

Outfits like this one have a limited product life—unless you go to a lot of costume parties!

Reducing Waste

If the world is not to slowly disappear under a mountain of waste, people must stop producing so much. There are several things they can do.

- Encourage manufacturers not to use unnecessary packaging.
- Recycle as much packaging as possible. Paper, cardboard, and many plastics, can be recycled instead of being thrown away.
- Shop for products that use packaging made of recycled materials.
- Say "no" to plastic bags and use cloth shopping bags instead.

The less packaging you use, the lighter your shopping footprint will be.

Choose Once, and Choose Well

"Choosing once, and choosing well" means:

- buying products that will last a long time, even if they cost more
- buying products that will not go out of fashion
- only buying products that are really needed and that will be used regularly

Buying only what you really need helps reduce the huge amount of waste produced by people.

Buying less is one of the best ways to have a lighter shopping footprint.

Case Study
Packaging Handbags

Some companies have come up with a surprising use for old potato chip bags and drink containers. They make them into handbags and shopping bags!

Discarded packaging is collected from the streets, cut open, washed, and dried. The old packages are then folded and sewn to make them into a stiff fabric, and stitched together using fishing line. The only nonrecycled part of the bag is the zipper used in some of them.

The packaging is different on every single bag, so each one is unique. The bags are brightly colored and, most importantly, have a tiny environmental footprint. Hardly any electricity or chemicals are used to make them, and because the bags are made from trash they do not use up any new resources.

BazuraBags™ are made from recycled materials that would normally find their way to the garbage dump.

How Big Is Your Shopping Footprint?

The size of your shopping footprint depends on how much shopping you do, and how and where the things you buy were made. How big do you think your footprint is?

Light Shopping Footprints

People whose shopping leaves light footprints on the environment think carefully about everything they buy.

- They do not buy anything they do not need.
- They do not replace things before they are worn out.
- They try to buy products that have been manufactured in ways that do not harm the environment.
- They buy products that have been transported as short a distance as possible.
- They buy products that can be recycled after they have worn out.

How big do you think your shopping footprint is?

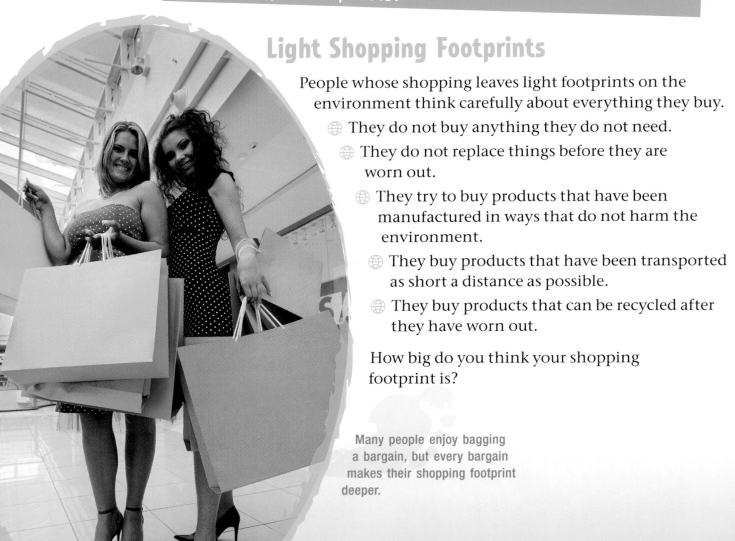

Many people enjoy bagging a bargain, but every bargain makes their shopping footprint deeper.

Sales encourage people to buy things they do not need.

Work Out Your Shopping Footprint!

On a piece of paper, make a note of how regularly ("never," "sometimes," or "often") you:

- travel to the store in a car
- go shopping without knowing exactly what you plan to buy
- buy clothes and wear them only for one season
- buy products because they are cheapest, without thinking about how long they might last
- put packaging straight into the trash, without sorting out the bits that can be recycled

If your answers are mostly "never," you have a light shopping footprint. Mostly "sometimes" means your footprints are average. But with a lot of "often" answers, you are treading heavily on the environment, and leaving very deep footprints.

Future Shopping Footprints

You can choose to take light footsteps or heavy footsteps. If people continue leaving heavy footprints, it could affect the environment for thousands of years to come.

What You Can Do

The Internet is a great way to find out more about what you can do to take lighter footsteps. Try visiting these websites:

- **http://www.worldwatch.org/node/1499**
  This site has all sorts of information about plastic bags and what you can do to reduce plastic bag use.

- **http://www.ecobusinesslinks.com/**
  This is a great site for information about all sorts of green businesses, from where to recycle your cell phone to how to harvest rainwater.

Some of the search terms you might use to find interesting information about shopping and the environment include:

- cotton irrigation
- environmentally friendly fabric
- organic clothing
- ecofriendly product.

Changing your shopping habits can be fun and environmentally friendly.

What will YOU do to change your shopping footprint in the future?

Glossary

artificial fibers
fibers that do not come directly from nature, but instead are made by humans, often using petrochemicals

developing countries
countries that are or have been poor, but are becoming wealthier

environment
the natural world, including plants, animals, land, rivers, and seas

evaporate
to change from a liquid to a gas

farmers' markets
markets where farmers bring their crops to sell directly to the public

fossil fuels
the remains of plants and animals from millions of years ago, which have been buried deep under Earth's surface and there turned into coal, oil, and gas

global warming
process by which Earth's average temperature is getting warmer over time

greenhouse gases
gases that are contributing to global warming, many of which are released when fossil fuels are burned

manufactured
made, or turned from raw materials into a product for people to buy and use

natural resources
natural substances, such as wood, metal, coal, or water, which can be used by humans

nonrenewable resources
resources that cannot be easily replaced, such as fossil fuels, which take millions of years to replace

organic farmers
farmers whose produce is grown without the use of artificial fertilizers or pesticides

packaged
wrapped up ready for people to buy in packaging such as cardboard boxes, plastic bags, cans, or foam cartons

pollution
damaging substances, especially chemicals or waste products, that harm the environment

recycling
treating the materials contained in a product so that they can be used again

renewable resources
resources that can be easily replaced

sewers
pipes and tunnels that carry away wastewater

transportation system
network of roads, railroads, airports, canals, and shipping routes that allows goods and people to be transported around

wages
money paid to someone for doing a job

Index